FEAST

INA CARIÑO

ALICE JAMES BOOKS
New Gloucester, ME
alicejamesbooks.org

CELEBRATING 50 YEARS OF ALICE JAMES BOOKS

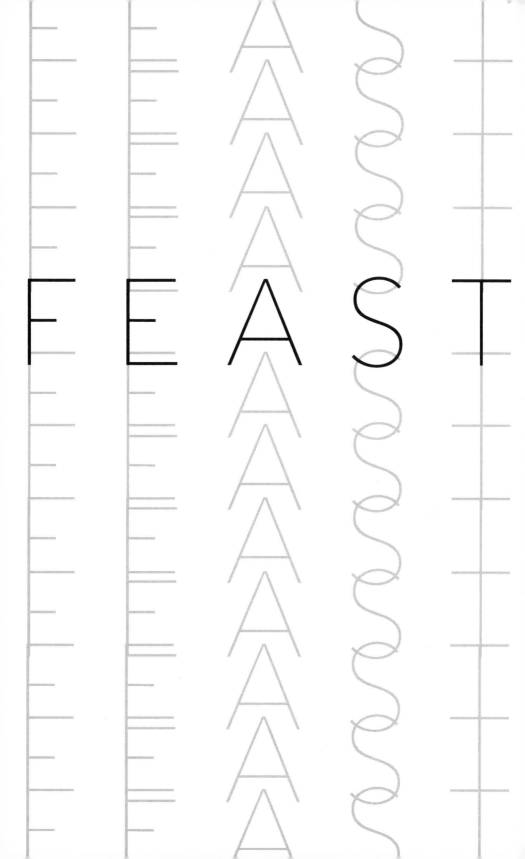

FEAST

10 9 8 7 6 5 4 3 2 1

Alice James Books are published by Alice James Poetry Cooperative, Inc.

Alice James Books
Auburn Hall
60 Pineland Drive, Suite 206
New Gloucester, ME 04260
www.alicejamesbooks.org

Library of Congress Cataloging-in-Publication Data

Names: Cariño, Ina, author.
Title: Feast / Ina Cariño.
Other titles: Feast (Compilation)
Description: New Gloucester, ME : Alice James Books, 2023
Identifiers: LCCN 2022034209 (print) | LCCN 2022034210 (ebook)
    ISBN 9781948579315 (trade paperback) | ISBN 9781949944273 (epub)
Subjects: LCGFT: Poetry.
Classification: LCC PS3603.A74775 F43 2023 (print) | LCC PS3603.A74775 (ebook)
    DDC 811/.6—dc23/eng/20220808
LC record available at https://lccn.loc.gov/2022034209
LC ebook record available at https://lccn.loc.gov/2022034210

Alice James Books gratefully acknowledges support from individual donors, private foundations, the National Endowment for the Arts, and the Amazon Literary Partnership. Funded in part by a grant from the Maine Arts Commission, an independent state agency supported by the National Endowment for the Arts.

Cover art: Photo Illustrations by Clarisse Provido; Photography by Yanran Xiong

CONTENTS

TAKIPSILIM

TAKIPSILIM

BITTER MELON

balsam pear. wrinkled gourd.
       leafy thing raised from seed.

pungent goya, ampalaya: cut
       & salt at the sink. spoon pulp

from bumpy rind, brown half-moons
       in garlic & sparking mantika.

like your nanay did. like your lola did.
       like your manang braving hot parsyak—

you'll wince. you'll think of the taste
       of your own green body—mapait

ang lasa. your sneer. masakit, dugo't
       laman. it hurts, this smack of bitter.

yes you'll remember how much it hurts,
       to nick your thumb as you bloom heat

in acid, sili at sukang puti—to grow up
       glowering in half-light—to flesh out

& plod through your own grassy way,
       unfurl your own crush of vines.

after you tip it onto a mound
       of steamed rice, as you chew,

the barb of it will hit the back
       of your throat. look at yourself,

square. you used to snarl at moths,
        start small blazes in entryways.

woodchip fires, flaking paint.
        look, tingnan mo—see your lip

curling in the glint of your bowl.
        unruly squash. acrid vegetable,

you'll flinch. you'll want to see
        nothing, taste like nothing. but

when you disappear your meal—
        when you choke on the last

chunky morsel of rice—you'll slurp
        thirsty for more—a saccharine life.

huwag mo akong kalimutan,
        you'll plead—

taste me.
taste me.

SOILED

with scrimshaw-handled comb,
double-sided butterfly, mama tends
to my hair—rakes fine-toothed wood

scarlet across my scalp, its spine
carved with peonies dappled gold.
the instrument glides easy enough

through oil-slicked locks, to sift
kuto: head lice, scourge of parents,
of every grade school classroom.

it is a collaborative effort, slow
hunt shared in swathes of sun
streaming past ikat curtains.

we count crawling parasites.
we pick the eggs with thumbnails,
liquid bug bodies still unformed.

edge pressed to keratin edge—
pop!—until the sacs burst & spray.
tiny teardrops, harmless.

sometimes, there is blood.
soon our lunar cuticles are dotted
with my own wet crimson.

//

I want to smear the same ruby shade
on my lips, jewel-chintz glinting
even at night. I want to click

down stairs, down sidewalks—
heels four inches high & cigarette-thin.
mama says I'm too young.

I still reek of playgrounds
at dusk, still rub heads with kids
whose kili-kili drip sweat

from scampering down alleyways,
past neighborhood sari-sari stores,
their cheap wares beckoning:

berry-colored Chinese Haw Flakes,
homemade lychee ice pops,
bags of chicharron for soaking

in suka at sili. my mouth
still withers pula, raisin-like
after sucking on the last

soggy pork rind—acid lifting skin,
edges curled. I suck & suck:
little louse puckering.

//

mama says I'll bleed soon.
nights, before bed, we read chapters
from a book naming things

that sound celestial—
cervix, vulva. labia majora.
she points on a diagram to a nub

in the middle, above an opening—
small guava pip waiting to grow.
I tell her I'm not afraid of red.

I'd skinned my knees before, felt plenty
strong when punched square in the gut
after calling a boy bobo, pangit.

putangina mo, he'd said, *your mother
is a whore*—& his fist hit swift,
trying to go straight through me.

I didn't even buckle. mama laughs,
whispers, *women bleed together.* no secret:
but I feel myself untethering, just as cord

was cut from womb—curse passed
down from daughter to daughter,
to daughter   to daughter.

LEAN ECONOMY

I pop tins of the greasiest luncheon meat open,
slather my chin with animal salt: asymmetrical
to the story of that soldier whose pinky fingers
were cut off in the war. want versus want.
real love is when you loot a crate of lard-filled cans,
throw it into the Pacific to feed your ancestors.
in this oily paradigm we learn to glut ourselves
on marrow. they say it's a shame I subsist
on scraps. *where do you shop for food?* show me
someone who won't argue that there's nothing
sentimental in this world, as if bastard histories
don't crave undoing. in exchange I'll show you how
to nourish yourself. lift your grandmother's knife.
slice through the fattest layer in your gut   & eat.

MILK

a brown sister told me someone told her   white people smell like milk
    so I took a good long whiff of one   brought him home with me

let him sleep in my bed   he kept me safe   kept me from lonely
    so I kept him from spoiling   from curdling   kept him

at night he dripped milk into me   my fingers gripping   his bony limbs
    my brown awash in milk   rinsed & cooled   I slurped it up

maybe he loved me   but only as white boys   love guavas
    from a warm country   pink-soft insides   fragrant other

maybe I loved him but only   as a brown girl   loves a white thing
    a so-called pure thing   makintab   a shiny lie   one day

I met his onion-skin mother   his candle-stump father   we talked
    about Asia   you know   that giant country   onion-mother said

my English was great   *no accent!*   candle-father said   I looked exotic
    are you—Polynesian?   they may as well have asked what it's like

to wake up smelling like dung   like tarantulas   burnt rice
    or flies in summer heat   smelling   like monsoon mildew   mud

stink bugs circling   instead they asked   if I'd tried dog   asked
    if I've ever once burned rice   because I must be so good at it

I don't need a recipe   they all laughed   so later that night
    I took my white boy to my lola's house   pulled down a jar

of black vinegar   sukang itim   dipped my tongue in it   kissed him
    you shoulda seen his pale face go see-through   chalk dissolving

reverse alchemy   now when I talk of white people   I tell my brown sister
        baho   they stink of milk   so I let mine go

she still shakes her head at me   says bobo   why are you so stupid
        says I was lucky   to be so close to one   who smells of milk

but when milk turns sour   ferments   blooms fetid under the nose
        the only thing to do is pour it   down the drain

TRIPTYCH WITH CITYSCAPE

Chicago, 2008

1.

in sweetrot city air
    I swallow pills
                for happy—
forget how to be a living
thing.
      my body's slow
decay smells
    of the fusty crush
of creatures jostling at dusk—
men & women
             crowding
the L as a charm of finches
flits
    overhead. in the hospital,
      watching the news,
building briefly ablaze
where people push hands daily
into fragrant:
          mustard,
          coriander,
          cumin—seeds
to fill gaps in my teeth.

2.

I'm a different kind of brute from what the man on the train thought—

     me facing the window as he asked

               how'd you get your hair to be so straight?

his reflection in plexiglass—dull form warped, grin crooked, coat

       stained with booze & upchuck. he stammered confused

           when I turned—but I was all mum-smiles

     as I got off at Hyde Park, where shiny condos swallowed shoddy brick.

   yes, I

always smile—even

        after papa scooped me up from the psych ward

   after Thanksgiving.

he warned me of a mother's shame, & I nodded.

               but I told him—

if you find me on a sidewalk, head in a puddle under a streetlamp,

   oil seeping into my sorry mouth—

        help me stand. tell me again

          of my mother & her name—

so that I might lift myself from concrete, shuck off

my pallid skin, & inhale—

exhale.

3.

I am lucky: my pulse mimics the slap
of sandals in gutter ponds where a child plays

under the spout of a hydrant. mornings,
I rise to windwhistle shrill between buildings.

Saturdays I slurp rice noodles, tofu skin,
in Chinatown—patina of hoisin sticky

under tongue. & nights, before burrowing
into sleep, I loose my hair from its flaccid coil.

so if I don't wake   if I fester lifeless
in my own muck, into feelers feasting—

it's because I've coddled my yearnings,
left my body spoiling in noonday heat: the kind

that leaves a mark even on the darkest part of me.

WHAT DOES DEATH FEEL LIKE
COMING FROM A WOMAN?

I walked before I crawled, refused
to splay limbs across dusty rugs,

& when yaya pinched my feet
I never flinched. then 1991—

mountain ashes cloudcrept into me
from Pinatubo's maw. my lungs

turned to wrinkled quinces,
while outside, lahar charred earth—

landscape raked, scorched
by encanto: a sylvan woman.

//

so mama said no running, afraid
for me: shriveled lansones, sickly.

threat of skinned shins. cherry
glow of lola's clove cigarettes,

smoke plumes sealing my throat.
or on my cheeks, plum rashes

blooming from playing in witch-
willow. these days, I don't run much.

but I was only seven when I broke
a girl's front teeth. was I cruel

//

I'd thought to take her for my wife.
she found a boy instead. so I bury myself

as star seed from caimito, always
under a scarlet dusk, as if pain makes me

special. as if the world knows I've only
been with men. I braid garlands

of a history I convince myself is real,
thread them jealous through my lover's hair.

I'd like someone to take me for her wife.
I always end up with a boy.

//

when I kiss a man in the park, fumble
awkward with his belt, I always finish.

I think I've grown up. mornings,
I touch myself, watch in the mirror

so I can pretend. still, my bones knock
unfamiliar in my rind—withering husk,

heaving. nights, I dream of woman,
a toothless diwata. she peels me

into scraps. siniguelas pip. cruel
damson stone. bruised remains: uneaten.

FEAST

I watch the slaughter—two men
drag a suckling, roped & squealing
across cement. I am five today,

hair tied in pigtails with ribbons,
barrettes in the shape of cherries
dangling at the ends. I scrunch

my eyes as they slit the hide—
pink bristle, wiry infant flesh—
can't help but gape at guts

that reek of insides I knew only
from dreams: gamey meat of mother,
ventricle & vein   ancient openings

waiting for the gush of new blood.
lolo says to eat is to be animal—
so they roast the little boar,

its skin turning crackling by fire.
when uncles lay it out on the table,
palm leaf platter underneath,

lolo takes a knife to its tongue
sticking out like dusk-red petal
from banana blossom. in a room

full of sweaty cousins, aunties floating
in chiffon, & maids hovering cautious
in the background to sweep up crumbs,

I stand in the center   starched
white dress loosely sheathing my frame.
for the gift of good speech, lolo proclaims,

& he slips cooked muscle
into my mouth, as if talking
were the means to something

only adults know. for dessert
I sit on mama's lap, & we feast
on buttery things: custard-yellow

brazo de mercedes, cream
of cashew sans rival, eggy yema
glazed with candied caramel.

from the back of my mouth, a splash
of bile washes my cheeks   & soon
I can't tell sweet from bitter, can't

remember how to swallow salt
the way a suckling in slaughter
must swallow its own briny tears.

WHEN THEY GLEAM, WHEN THEY CLATTER

your first loose milk tooth snapped   from wiry gumvein
        wet pearl tumbling into palm   as you stood in the garden

you'd pulled & pulled till tissue tendril untethered   & clumpy clots
        seeped   crimson ink blotting   your bottom lip

you thought *this is what it's like*   *to bleed*   to pour out   to press
        detached incisor onto finger pads   grubby

you cradle-cupped the fang in jam hands   put it in a jar   rattled it
        ringing   to fluster the maya   chirping in the durian tree

but lolo snatched the thing   hid it under rafters for luck
        you shrieked   trilled indignant   but he just laughed

nights after   a dream of molars   falling from your mouth
        & you recalled the old warning: when you dream

of rotting teeth   chew on old wood   or someone you love
        will pass away   but you told no one   sneered sour

at broom handles   used matches   lola's cracked rosary
        its beads carved from an olive tree that once grew in Bethlehem

soon lolo took ill   his canines jutted   tips protruding like aswang
        ashen   & when he died   moths clustered over his casket

ghostly bouquet   *this is what it's like to kill*   to cause to die
        to snuff a life quick   & you recalled the old saying:

when white moths gather   the dead flutter among them
        so you smudged candle wax   coaxed it into the shape of wings

thorax   abdomen   took storm-fallen branches   bit hard
        till splinters barbed your tongue   you tried to undream

float your milk tooth from the roof   to nestle it safe
        in your mouth   & snatch it   snatch it all back

SHINGLES

n. A painful rash caused by the reactivation
of the varicella-zoster virus, which also causes chickenpox.

I pluck jewels from my grandmother's back—
     violet/red in their hardening, dotting her scapula,
her spine. spurious blossoms surround them,

     burnished patches. I ask if she is in pain,
& she murmurs *no*—she facing the altar in the corner
     of the bedroom, statues of Mary & Joseph

dusty on the ledge. grandmother is a woman of red.
     carnival-red lipstick, vermilion stilettos,
crimson chiffon as she sashays in ballrooms.

     mothball musk wafts from cherry-red handbags
hanging in the closet. rubies bulge around her throat.
     now her skin itself blushes that pulsing hue.

still a child, I find nothing strange about pressing
     my hand onto her bare vertebrae, her nakedness
just another way of being in the world. & I can't

     tell she is hurting. she must have stood
straight just days after her hysterectomy in 1967,
     when doctors razored her appendix out

at the same time—two in one go. hysterikos,
     from the womb   such women of red,
called crazed for snarling at their husbands.

     I wipe her skin with a hot damp cloth. after,
she lies down on the bed, not even getting under the covers,
     her henna-dyed curls now streaking white.

& I pull the blanket over her, can't see her face as she heaves
        silent, shudders into sleep. the thing about sores:
unlike jewels, unlike rouge smeared onto cheeks,

        they decorate the body like scars—
        wounds pretending to be badges from war.

WATCH ANIMALS CLOSELY FOR STRANGE BEHAVIOR

Luzon, 1990. Fatalities: est. 1,621.

after the quake
    to remind you flight was never meant to be forever
your mother will gift you a pocketful
    of broken feathers
            an apology of fading stars
what might otherwise be mistaken for daylight
    you'll have bolted your furniture
    installed latches on cabinets
    learned doorways are no stronger than any other part of a building
        but your father will have taught you
    to carry a sack of centavos
burlap cradling coins to feed both living & dead
    after the quake practice being less than quiet
  to shrug silent
    to unexist
      to step lightly over figures who wear your sister's clothes
those limp things lining street gutters
          fractured
          shoeless
after the quake boys whose soles are pricked with glint-glass will gather at your house
      though you'll have hung wreaths woven
    from the hair of elders
  silver above windows to ward off looters to whom you'll tell stories with no words
because everyone should know
         what a mouth with no tongue sounds like
      it won't be long until colors won't matter
        what shadow shapes do you see when no one is in sight?
        what does a tree look like what does a church look like
  what does God   look like
        after the quake be cautious

watch animals closely for strange behavior

extinguish small fires

& follow trails of flies to find the faceless under rubble

who would have thought a city could run out of caskets

who ever thought about caskets needing linings

silk or brocade to cradle puffed arms & legs

where will the wood come from where will the nails come from

after the quake

to remind you flight was never meant to be forever

what's left of your cousins will put makeshift coffins together from tarp & old wood

stuff them with limbs

fling them off cliffs to be buried

ULAN

TERRIBLE BODIES

1.

we began in soil   mountain-
roughed   soursop-smeared.

candles in the cabinets—
matches plastic-wrapped
for when typhoons bring dank.

we feed ourselves luxury—
lard slopping out of tin cans.

no room for mimicries—
history : its invasions : perverted
repetitions   death marches

hill stations   conquistadors.
but we watch the sun come up

think it's down in reverse. news
of terrible brown bodies
shunted. still   this wish:

that the world's full blossoming
might unhinge such absurd thievery.

2.

to be other is to read badly-
drawn maps.

our brown breasts want
for thrum—

for curve of rib
to hum

with a revolutionary's
love song.

3.

oh how the milk-stained
                    hush. remind them
           of Dogtown, USA:
                los Indios Bravos forced
   into false homes   replicas. made
                         to eat mutt
  be mutt   spit
             -snarl muzzled   that fascist gag.

  remember—marrow
               nourishes best coaxed
  from familiar crevice—
             sweet bone. tender
      on the tongue—
            our own canine muscles.
  bitten inner cheek. in this way
           we taste ourselves.

4.

taste mother taste father   bitter
as herbs from a bastard country.

do not bend. be as narra heartwood
culled for its burl. be as fissured nib—

ink your terrible body onto paper:
that whitest of worlds.

I SING DESPITE THE TENDER STENCH OUTSIDE

anthems tells me more than
the throbbing of this country,
& when only my shadow listens, I
carry this curtain of hair
warbling. my slow step's
quaver, loping
speed—crawling—
a child.
turned inside out,
my inhale stops short—
a more capable machine,
lit up on screens.
money feigns, will wring
music bitter taut.

my waking life:
tempo charred by bigotry.
lick sand from my lips.
from one hill to another,
still catching up—
toward replicated homes,
a necessity.
what is an anthem
in crisis.
I breathe, a dusty concertina—
interpret sweat as if it were
a farewell wheeze—
a ratty flag:
elegies fail.

dirges for
sister-flocks darker than.
my freckles
mimic my mother's
elbows, brown awls,
jostled kneecaps.
I am scampering,
but a love song
in dreams.
the wrong listeners hear
a film burn, negatives
not an option.
the old guard will make
even crumbs nourish.

MY CHILDHOOD IS A COUNTRY
OF THIEVES —

false saints donning Spanish
brocade capes   to rob me rancid

they stifle dappled beetles
pour candle wax on my anthems
papa's harana turns to loam

panoply of drug wars   skulking
in Barangay 106—red nacre
plumes of shit & fishball stink

they say the best thieves secret
their crimes through art   say
poets are not fit to be war heroes

film reel silhouette: a child's
laugh   collateral damage
as face crimps to blankest stare

still I dream of the plaster Santo Niño
phantom-eyes blinking through paint—
I pity poets   (both children & thieves)

& when no one looks
both poets & children grieve
the shifting contours

of cathedrals
elders' sumpâ
rusty centavos mistaken for home.

& I have witnessed the dusk jasmine
blooming from holes
in a dead boy's chest.

to be a thief is to unstick the plastic glow-in-the-dark stars from the ceiling.
to be a poet is to write about the hollows that take their place.
to be a child is to love what's left:

a country full of thieves
a ceiling full of holes
saints who only dream of pilfered beauty.

SNAPSHOTS OF GIRL WITH GALAXY OF SPIDERS DROWNING IN SOPAS

I'm bone-child on a stool   stripping longbean spines for pay   snapping stem   from crisp green
body   mackerel on the stove   bawang at suka   peppercorn   bay leaf   I hum over
the milkscent   of bubbling rice   & on the back burner   broth at rolling boil   simmering
gingered with—stars : tiny   charcoal bituin bobbing   on the surface   I stir the pot on tiptoe
dots swim   frantic   miniature cogs   little brood spinning   into their own deaths   what brought
you here straight   from nest?

//

I toss the lot   hatchlings & all   sayang   pero there's the beans   there's the fish   & before
the family sits at table   I sneak stewed cheek   with slotted spoon   careful not to forget the pearl
cradled   in eye socket   maalat at maasim   brackish   sour   fat lining skeleton slips easy   into
my mouth   I slurp   suck it clean   spit white sphere onto palm where it goads   *take the other
one*   so I pinch jellied meat   scrape it with teeth jagged   jutting   until tongue finds little curve
& I swallow it by mistake

//

that night I dreamed   of dying stars   silver isda winding canals   in my gut   searching for
their cousin's eye   dead nova   but the globe was gone   dissolved   by the sour soup of my
own   green body   fragrant as mud   good brown earth   insect-leaf   sediment   soil   oh
what alchemy   & instead of metal to gold   it was calcium to acid   magnesium to water   chalk
to oil   I wanted to be as world outside   as oceanscape   universe in small kernel   but waking
I rubbed crust from lashes   looked : in the mirror   soot girl   stick girl   sweeping-the-steps-
with-walis-ting-ting girl   girl tinik-thin   straight from her nest   left with her marrowless bones

WHEN I SING TO MYSELF, WHO LISTENS?

no good people   in my house
        want to live   we schedule
little quakes   on Sundays
        on the steps   broken glass
after mass   I prefer
        to stay here   pero
I never asked for   this
        a song strummed   I listen:
such beauty   music soft
        demure   papa's harana
mama—paraluman   his muse
        she croons   of better yesterdays
floor giving way   to earth

//

        I'm of earth   so sick
    so sick   I lap soap
        I wash my face   imagine soil
    pushing   up
        as maya finches flit   in the garden
    mornings   I wash salt
        from my body   ibon! ibon!
    perched   in magnolia
        (stay with me)   (is that wrong?)
on good days   I'm nothing—
        like mama   tremors start
    nobody stays   which is wrong

INTAKE

Lakeshore Hospital, 2008

Identifying information:

    in the mirror   shadow-hair
    thighs swollen as dripping langka

    & I remember my city of moss
    how my night-beak was muzzled

    by strangers who took my bra away
    I guess I'm a statistic now

    it makes me walk funny but
    I can still say my mother's good name

History:

    once I took a hot iron to my chest
        little ginger-plank girl brooding
            at a window in front of a busy street—

    imagined my reflection engulfing red
        jeepneys & rickshaws hurtling straight
            between my legs   black fuzz teeming

    once   I was able to enjoy sunlight
        catching on a man-made lake
            I was curious about how rain soaks

    into soil   sometimes I read stories
        about plundering   & these days
            I sleep alone (though I love many)

Presenting problems:

I am moments away from fission.
I am unaware of the loss it surely brings.

Do you currently take any medications? Please list them all:

mornings I wake to the sound of my lola frying eggs in the kitchen. I listen to the pop of mantika spraying on her arms, remember she is dead.

at noon I sit on the porch, feed on the breeze under beetle wings.

evenings I forage a feast for the body, skim fat from yesterday's soup for tomorrow's stew. woodears grow in the sinews of trees (they taste of fragrant dirt).

during monsoon I push my hands through the window. I think the squalls are made-up, but thunder's only frightening when it's real.

Do any cultural or social factors affect treatment?

sometimes
when I make love
I am surprised
when my left hand
reaches out
touches my right

YOU DREAM OF SAINTS

somnambulist they call you:
sleepwalker—always specter-eyed
in the morning, doors & windows

still locked from inside. you know
walking through walls isn't normal.
does your sickly flesh dissolve?

melt into, through concrete?
still, you can't help it—
you dream upright regardless.

//

Novena to Our Mother of Perpetual Help: Nine Wednesdays

you are a little girl again, grass-
stained palms sticky jam-mouth.
lolo watches the novena on TV:

in Baclaran, Parañaque City,
a stone virgin cries red tears, cracked
face greasy from being touched—

eyes staring hollow on the screen.
tita shrieks so you follow suit—
but lolo shushes you, intones deep-

voiced: *loving Mother pray for us—*
& for never-ending Wednesdays after,
he drags you to mass at night.

soon you'll be confirmed. dalaga
ka na. should you confess
your sins? like how you pushed

blood into blood? pulled flesh
from aching flesh? as in—you pressed
fingers into your own crevices. as in—

you pulled them out, licked them
clean on humid afternoons,
moisture film of phantom skin.

Simbang Gabi: Night Mass

is that grandmother's altar cloaked
in the smoke of snuffed candles?
half asleep, you trudge to the bathroom,

get ready for the long dawn ahead.
Christmas—that Spanish custom.
papa told you about 1669:

how farmers compromised with clergy
to pray before the workday started,
instead of after their bodies turned raw

from tilling land in December sun.
on the 24th at midnight, lola makes
things from rice: rainbow-hued puto,

glutinous bibingka, sweet suman
in banana leaves—food to fill stomachs
for cheap. mama warms tsokolate

on the stove to temper acrid papait,
the goat bile bubbling slow
in a covered pot. you can't eat it

without wincing. the grown-ups
know bitter is good for you, good
for growing, for growing up.

Feast of the Santo Niño: January

your mama calls from the iron gate.
you trip, scrape elbows, rusty
rivulets running down arms.

looking at the sky you see
shadow-shapes promising rain
& up the road: Santo Niño being

carried down the hill. old women
warble as they take him inside,
set young saint on marble stand.

you swear he looks at you funny.
you'd already collided with
enchantment: fears of dwende

in tree roots & hungry aswang,
swinging. they snatch in the dark,
take scrappy little brats like you—

feed on them. after prayers
the room empties & you go to him:
child Jesus—stare into painted pupils

until he blinks at you—winks—
smiles terrible. in waking life you wail,
grubby in the shrubs in the yard—

//

shins bramble-scratched,
soggy socks streaked with mud.
you crawl to the front door,

find it locked tight. your body
throbs, cold from the frost
on the ground. you think you hear

your mother calling. you think
you   are mother—
you think   you are calling.

YESTERDAY'S TRAUMAS, TODAY'S SALT

my family dines luxurious—peasant food in crystal bowls:
seven thousand six hundred forty-one islands jostling in my soup.

here is Luzon, Visayas, Mindanao—grandmother points to mounds
dunking up & down in the saltbroth. *& rice, don't forget the rice,*

which she steamed in the old palayok—earthen pot & lid,
unglazed red clay lending its savage tang to the soft white.

grandmother makes the sign of the cross. *archipelago is just another word*
for slaughtered, amen, & I chomp on palmfuls of dirt, grease rivering

down my neck—push rice into my open maw. remnants of
a sepia life slosh in the silt of my stomach. because my stolen body

is still burdened with salt, my tongue pinched with its bite, I salt
bitter gourd, drown it in vinegar. I salt fish bellies to dry under sun.

I salt the rice heavy when the meat is low, to trick my stomach
out of hunger. my muscles still remember old aches—as if suspended

in the salt of an ocean I crossed alone. how much can the body take?
a certain kind of pain, this accumulation of salt. I was named anguish

before I was born, crooked teeth crowd my mouth, my fangs rake ash
& soil. will I die when the muck hits my bloodstream. yes I salt, keep—

tuck things away—coins still line the hems of my grandfather's coat.
I clamor at the sight of salt spilled, grit skidding under broom spindles.

but I pucker from too much salt, fingers withered, oldest ginger. tongue
brined, voice washed by white—my name flapping out of my mouth—

an unfamiliar moth. its chalkwings dust my chin as I swallow
seven thousand six hundred forty-one islands: the only home I know.

RICE

unhatched songs   quiet perfumed white
dirt-born pips cooking on the stovetop

I listen in half-light   breathe still   tilt my ear
as memories of lola float up with the milkscent

over her shallow basket she'd clean the rice
pick tan shell from ivory kernel   say

in America   with a husk like that
you could scuff at the lightest skin   the palest fear

daily she fed me   sweet muck of thick soy
gingered meat   hot mounds of rice

I still wonder how a grain too small for a wish
holds the task of feeding in its shell

I left lola on her cement step   her chipped
plates   those women stooped & bronzing in paddies

& I try not to confuse the smell of soggy hulls
with the damp musk of an American Dream

still I wait for the water to bubble in the pot   & soon
in this half-light they'll bud up soft   be what they'll be

& when it's time to grow up into this white
white world   give me a brown husk like that

TO THE BOY WHO WALKS BACKWARDS
EVERYWHERE HE GOES

1.

tacit slow,
gangle-limb-pillar—
you could have been any age,
    & you followed me reverse
    in your grubby sweater-vest,
  heels sliding & scuffing beige carpet.
      I wondered why
          you moved wrong
         through this padded world—
why your brown hands didn't swing
        back & forth
     as you trudged around
        the funny ward.

2.

      soon I learned everyone here moved   in wrong
                  directions.
    the girl down the hall flailed against her coat
        instead of sleeping in it.
the firefighter with a plan wept, in the end—drew me
    a rainbow. & nights,
      the doctor had me swallow
        capsule cure-alls for being awake.
      but that first day when the nurse took away
    my pilled bra   you peeked sideways
          past polyester curtains,
      thick-rimmed glasses catching
     green & yellow under fluorescent light.
    I couldn't see   your eyes.

3.

on the fourth day I rang up my mother
                   on the black hallway rotary,
        & she scolded shrieking. I hung up,
turned round the corner: you were there, witness
      to my baffled tears. at last, your eyes—
                 had you
    been facing me on purpose?
you nodded deliberate   mouthed something
                 undecipherable with chapped lips.
      suddenly I knew: the only thing different
    between you & me was how we'd been taught
          to survive, how
       to announce our arrival.

4.

     last
     Thursday   Thanksgiving. you & I
  shared a meal: dry
             turkey   green beans
              potatoes mealy from a box.
      the others snatched at extra milk cartons, but we
             were still,
         content
  with one each, ice chunks
    slow-melting
         in their soggy white boxes.
  but I can't wait till snow turns
to grey slush outside,
    which means they might let me go,
 finally.
if I sign that special form
       & papa picks me up before sundown,
    forgive me for leaving   forgive me
   for not taking you with me   for running
       the right way.

RITUAL FOR SICKNESS

I am ill again. lola warms milk
& sugar on the stove,

pours it into a small teacup, tips
an egg yolk onto the white skin

that formed while she cracked
the shell in two. I down it all

in one hot swallow. *here,* she says,
follow the river that drowns eggs

in the night. she traces a path
down my throat, my chest,

across my rib. my haggard breaths
fog the windowpane by my bed.

I imagine the yellow globe
sloshing around in my gut.

wait for the sac to burst, she says,
to coat the lining of your stomach.

but my breaths remain jagged.
I slip into a haze, drift

from one current of blanket
to another. still, the final step—

to change my name, confuse
the spirits who bring sickness.

come inside this newly invented light.
so I pull on my wool socks, stagger

to the mirror, lock eyes with the girl I see:
her black hair clings to sallow skin.

I am not who I am, she intones.
I am like you—ghostly, a specter.

soon after, I retch the cream
into the toilet bowl. the acid

of curdled liquid soaks my tongue
as my belly is emptied & cleansed.

MAKAHIYA

n. Diffusely spreading half-woody fernlike plant. The "shy" plant.
The leaves are sensitive, folding inwards when touched.

I am the wilting herb
leaves bruised   the shame-
plant   *Mimosa pudica*

weak vine   creeping
grass—   trace a finger along
my spine   & I'll shiver

I am the bashful one   waif
shaking   in my inner life—
once   I birthed sprouts

& weeds   dandelion clocks—
making wrong   knowing sin
I pulled them out   still

I am the waking root
gnarled   giving
plentiful—   I wait

in wet earth where tendrils
touch: finger to capillary
& evenings   before darklight

thrushes in trees weep—
I shut the door   no tears
for me   but I've felt

the weight of soft flesh
leave my body—   I wash
my hands   at night

BALINTATAW

ASOCENA

aso, n., Tagalog: dog

cena, n., Spanish: dinner

in the town   mutts crowd cabbage fields
blanketed white in the plush crust of frost.

mama thrums dream-songs—the placental calms
as you gum her pink nipple—steeps you

in the hushed sounds of home: papa wiping
windows with yesterday's *SunStar* newspaper

& yaya flouncing crib sheets laundered, damp
on the stair railing, drying;   but outside

nobody knows how to live in this cold—
how to keep the bones warm in this cold.

you are a wan child, but hound blood cures the most
feversick   so tito strangles a dog from behind—

gags the mouth with rough rag so it won't bite,
hammers lumber & nail into the skull.

lola will slice the lean flesh for a pan simmer—
garlic & soy—serve it with gulay:

orange kabocha, vinegared beans,
ampalaya bitter as iron behind the teeth.

from womb to river we swim with coins under tongues—
but when the crops are gone, dogs will still roam.

heart muscle rends even under the dullest blade,
so mama will dribble milk & marrow into your mouth.

you'll grow up strong, palpable fruit. steaming
stubborn as ice under rain—a wild soiled thing.

INTERDISCIPLINARY

Winter Quarter, 2008
Student ID: 10381939

doctors think I'm self-
           suspended   body as fossil crumbling,
           sepia spray of drifting dust—undeclared.
      as in, I have no discipline.

Chicago, ill   in these musty wards—
        men scribble on pads. I clutch my chest,
maroon t-shirt grime,
     white block letters archeological:
               WHERE FUN GOES TO DIE—

      can I be healed by syrup swell?
        can I be pill-fed
     & still in-
          finitely be?

haven't showered, afraid for my particle
                     form. as if sweat
        shields me from residents who ogle
        my grease-sheen & straggle-locks.

    but when the girl down the hall secrets me
soap & shampoo from her stash, silky
        white in a pink plastic dosing cup, I cave
& lather my hair, my face,
    this slick flesh.
          theory: test
        credits apply   but only
for 10381939 selves.
       yes I'm ill—& still
    I am biological.

                    the purpose of the dig—
              to jig artifact into light,
       dust off soil / ash.
              make porous bones gleam again—

buzz their memories   hum lush from hollows,
                 calcium stories uncrushed. know this:
       my marrow will never be obsolete.

WHEN A WOMAN IS UGLY

when a woman is ugly she roams
under strangler figs that choke the trees
along Balete Drive, Quezon City.

call her multo, ghost sheathed
in ivory silk, ether dragging
on the ground. rumor is,

she was raped & killed along this road.
cabbies on the graveyard shift swear
she is beautiful—but the kind of beautiful

that calls to mind the final swell
of red hibiscus growing in ditches.
in the taxi, suddenly she is bruised

& bloodied, suddenly she is ugly—
like a woman is ugly in full fright:
mouth rimmed with froth, spittle-

foam dribbling down her neck—
all animal-eyes, roving   desperate.
if an ugly woman stops you on the road,

dig for her bones under the biggest balete,
its vines smothering the mother tree
underneath. evenings, the wood plies

soft, for a moment bending
from the day's residual heat.
yes, when a woman is ugly,

her limbs extend: crooked branches
casting shadows over asphalt—sobs
under the noise of passing cars, unheard.

PIYESTA

Feast: n. A large meal, typically held as a celebration.
From Vulgar Latin festa (also source of Spanish "fiesta").

1.

surrendering to a new tongue
    is having mine sliced
                on the jag of expectation:
      language cut on sweetened rim—
chipped teeth whitened.
                but sugar burns bitter. I watch
        my sentences crack   candy glass
            shattering on foreign floors.

2.

as a child only the sweetest poisons would do
    to nettle my mouth electric. once I swallowed

a tamarind hard candy, the size of a large marble,
    whole. it slunk down my esophagus, bulged

& stuck itself halfway, so I ran away from yaya
    thinking myself heathen—bound to be in trouble

for the accidental gulp. in my tempest-blinking,
    she called my name, found me under the banister,

her hands warm & blurred as I wept. *matay akon—*
    this is how I die. but instead of letting me,

she had me polish the hardwood floors
    with a dried coconut half, push on the husk

with my foot. we did it together—better than wax.

soon the candy melted within the house of my ribs.

3.

these days I crave salt

over sweet   shiver

at the sting of it

threshing my inner

cheeks—

pucker of gums   swollen bottom lip

as I swallow soups

& stews: peasant food

from sepia days   vegetables swimming.

gristle meets tooth in the vinegar

dance of my mother's   mother. but

when century eggs stare dark   those jellied eyes,

I mash orange kalabasa into my rice,

ready to honey bitter bile ladled

purposeful   into every red clay bowl

4.

when typhoons flapped torrential above the crags of the Cordillera & the power went out, my mother
would slip wool warmers onto my legs, bundle me in mothball sweaters & dappled ikat shawls.
we'd light candles around the house, procession of dripping tapers: my sisters' necks garlanded by
everlasting strawflowers—candy scent so slight even years after they'd dried. such rituals—board
games in the dark, shrimp chips & boiled peanuts at dawn. in the end, even immortal flowers shed
petals like tears, the straw-daisies strung around our necks gilding the way to a new country.

5.

to eat is to meld tongue with heat.
an abundance of crumbs at table—
milky mounds of pan de sal   bible

tripe drowning in gravy. pair the best
parts of harvest with the worst:
longbeans with okra mottled, crisp

onion to counter the softest parts
of a nightshade's skin. the flesh of it—
sweet. I pinch the cream with fingers,

burn the expectant roof of my mouth,
as if waiting for the pain that makes me
whole again, alive: nabiag ak.

WHEN I SAY HELLO TO THE OLDEST APPLES

they tell me
a mountain is good for me. disowned by my papa,
I don't reply—afraid of fathers, decades of dirt.

my cousins would sneer & slop me wet rice—
no mercy for a curse of daughters instead of sons.
a family tree scattered. spit in my tea.

maybe I am unloved because I want to deal
in the currency of ghosts—to traffic in such
precious things as broken rosaries, jars of ash.

when I ask for pardon as I trample knotted roots,
I nod to the spirit inside the wood: dwende, old
man of the mound who snatches bad children.

dirty one, you can't walk here. I confess, I am
a dirty one. in dreams my claws rake the soil
of my mama's garden as I search for fallen figs.

my brow ignores its lineage, tries to forget
centuries of grey-eyed Spaniards lurking
my veins, knocking the lumber of my heart.

when I say goodbye to manzanitas, boughs withering,
they tell me I'll never forget them, that I'll never
find fruit as familiar as their ripest berries.

I climb these trees, but in dark churches, hot wax
drips my knob-knees, sweat skimming the velvet
back of my neck. I can't let go of what I think

is still mine—bloodlines flooding the slopes
of the Cordillera, silver in the hills—pine sap
casing my teeth as I say hello to the oldest apples.

NAMES ARE SPELLS, & I HAVE FOUR—

the first to tether me to a man
called my father. the second
for grace, the third for foraging
with finches. the last, silence—
a thrush in the mouth, something
precious I can't touch. a broken
name, & what is chanted broken
is holy. am I broken, am I worthy
& real. *tutoong Cariño ka?*
tao ako—I'm real. I honey
my tongue with hands dreaming
of family ghosts. split lips—stung
petals, armor. I remember cold
women staring as I sucked
on melting red berries. I know
they spelled me, named me *not.*
not now, not ever part of. but
I am not *never.* I am as mother
in a marrow tongue, as mirror
spurning shadows into fractals.
I thought to spell my name
with flight, to whisper shameful
pleas to an unforgiving god. but
I know my name bloating
into furious sugar could never
burn bitter. yes I name myself. I am
the last spell, the only song left.
deliberate utterance of bone.

I DREAM IN A TONGUE OTHER THAN MY OWN

one minute I'm tweedy smack / and the next I'm banjo-twang / yes one minute I'm angle-whip / and the next I'm eliding endings / with beginnings / mouthing vowels so flat my mongrel self / sounds almost real / but I dream in a different dialect / sift my mother's stout syllables / plump honorifics / from the language of my colonizers / what is left? / glossy contractions / shiny / subjunctive / grammar that belongs / to the anthropology of the pale / people who look nothing like me / my lips / inflamed / form these words / my throat forced to swallow syntax / cheeks lined / with the hook & barb / of prepositions for proper / we / creatures broken / domesticated / blistered maws muzzled / my brown body a vessel / torched / suffused with the idioms of my invaders / white bodies with alien speech who are alarmed / by the rolling / smacking / slapping of tongues on crooked teeth / my croon a fire / my throat a chimney / my tongue as white / as a flag burning / burning / my tongue / is burning is / burning my tongue / is burning / is burning / is

INFINITIVES

	to speak	to sing	to be
simple past	once we buzzed & babbled, content amid the gum-soft jostle of maya finches— in the eaves, beetles— roosters in the yard	at school I hummed the canticles of Spaniards, warbled white— yearned for syncopations to disrupt the steady plod of American hymns	we learned to fold our lips, purse slurps around fleshy slivers of fat, around animal tendons grease-gleaming at the joints
simple present	these days we mutter charms, soak our cheeks with prophecies: words to shield our children from the tragedy of being born brown	evenings, I spit prayers to a foreign god— wail a hair too sharp, a quarter click too slow against such a rigid metronome	we know how to strip a suckling bone clean— know how to leave nothing, not even the juice of bulalo in the cracks
simple future	we will gift them stories of encanto, of babaylan— decorate our sentences with tumid moss & woodear mushroom— won't we? won't we?	who's to say what I will chant in the face of pale & proper? I'll sift honorifics, pluck syllables from the branches of lola's garden: opo—opo	we'll whistle in fractured color, fill fissures with birdsong from the hills—salve for wounds sustained splicing our tongues

PERISHABLE

for Mama Tet

my grandmother taught me how to slit
the milky belly of my favorite fish. to scrape
at filmy scales with a knife, snip the stiff fins
behind each gill. I watched as her hands,
cracked & mapped with grease scars,
lifted the flap of its stomach under running
water: green viscera awash in vermilion,
streaming down the drain. slashed body—ready
for the pan, for salted skin to spark in oil.
it was dark in our kitchen, a single window
above the sink, & I didn't understand
what perishable meant. once, at school,
we were tasked with gathering canned goods
for people devastated by typhoon.
beans, instant coffee, tins filled with rice.
I wanted to send them bananas. eggs, butter,
sayote. milkfish, what I knew of sustenance.
but grandmother let me be. I packed the dying
treasures in a cardboard box—took them
to class the next day. everyone laughed.
in shame I cracked the eggs behind a bookshelf
to sulfur the hall in the weeks to come. I knew
that much—that breaking can mean release.
what I didn't know was that the fish
under the faucet wasn't alive, even as
I'd watched grandmother hook her finger
into its cavity & pull from the wound.
at dinner, I poked at cooked flesh with my fork,
a million bones fine as whiskers threatening
to prick my gums. *why didn't you tell me.*

grandmother didn't answer. instead she pried
spine from remaining half, picked the meat clean
of tines—scooped it soft into my mouth.

CHIMERA

once   you told me
I could be ugly
when I wanted

hair dismal
damp   mournful—
mouth a dark

nook under
a tree where
night badgers

crickets
bat-eared foxes
hide—

you said I
could be
dreadful

angry fistful
of thorns stripped
from the stems

of roses—
the red & green oils
flowing from

the gutted belly
of a fish   or a squirrel's
swollen form   frozen-

fallen from a tree
seething with worms
white as rice

black nights
know my name—
when you say it

you hear candles
being snuffed   I want
to be as those curls

of smoke
but to want
is not to have

& what I have
is only my likeness
in the mirror

so I could
be gone if you
wanted

the way you wash
the day's salt
off your hands

BIRTHSTONE

on days when I feel more like a woman
      than a man, I remember that my mother
            keeps a brown nub buried in her jewelry box,

under strings of pearl & heaps
      of mountain silver. little heart, wrinkled—
            remains of my umbilical cord, tucked

in a small leather coin purse—nestled
      in folds of rice paper, dotted with spots
            of its oil. this once-conduit: dermis crusted—

the death of flesh, exemplified. as a child,
      I begged to see it, balked at the funk, prodded it
            with the pillow of my fingertip, gentle.

when I asked her why she preserved it,
      like a prune, she just laughed & said something
            about keeping me close until she dies.

you'll understand, when you're a mother.
      now, I am of childbearing age. mornings,
            I stare at my handsome face in the mirror

as I check for lumps in my breasts. on such days,
      when I feel more like a man than a woman,
            I wince at the thought of being a mother.

& on days when I don't feel like a woman
      or a man, I think about the brown nub that,
            for a time, connected me to my own—

imagine how it might now crumble, after years
      buried in her jewelry box. maybe tomorrow
            I will call her, ask about the little heart.

HIBISCUS DREAM NO. 4

little one, find me on the roadside   crest
                    of hill: gumamela blush.
      pulp me   mash stamen
                    & pistil—petals deep red.
      then, in a glass jar   slosh me with water
                    till I'm viscous,
        juice turned thick.   you'll twist a thin metal rod,
& coil it until a loop forms.
                    or, you'll use an old plastic wand
          left over from a bottle
      of bubble mix bought with coins
                    stolen   from your lola's purse.
    yes, I know—your sisters did
                    as you do now.
                    they licked the air
            tongues flicking, feelers searching
        for someone to love them whole.
                    when you blow the slime sap of me
          through the small hoop—
                    what wonder on your grub-face,
    what whimsy in your fingers,
                    sticky from the stuff that seeps
      from filament   ovary.
                    when the bubbles pop—
                    when the concrete stoop is soaked,
    patterned   with small wet circles—
            will you search for me again
        among verdant fronds?   tell me
                    you need me   tell me stories
          of how diwata women
      pluck me entire, sepal up,
                    their mallow hands mothering.
or at least, wear me behind
                    your ear—& gift me to those

who know you best: your lolo,

his stone grave cold. your mama,

bold, unafraid. encanto—

enchanted ones who roam free.

IT FEELS GOOD TO COOK RICE

it feels good to cook rice
it feels heavy to cook rice
it feels familiar
                good

    & *heavy*   to cook rice

            when I cook rice
        it is because hunger is not just
                an emptiness
but a longing   for multo:
                    the dead who no longer linger

        two fingers in water
        I know just when to stop:
        right under the second knuckle

in the morning   chew it
                        with salted egg
in the evening   chew it
                        with salted onion
at midnight   eat it
                        slovenly
        with your peppered hands   licking
relishing   each cloudmorsel

                    sucking greedy   as if
        there will no longer be any such thing
as rice

            good
        is not the idea of pleasure
                    rather
                    it is the way
                        I once tripped

                    spilled a basket
of hulls & stones onto soil—
homely sprinkle of husks
as if for a sending off—
            how right it was: palms
            brushing the chalk of it
            swirls rising in streaking sun

        heavy
is not the same as burden
                    rather it is falling rice
                        as ghostly footfalls—
                    trickling mounds
                            scattered on wood—
my dead lolo in compression socks
my dead lola in red slippers scuffing
& a slew of yesterday's titos & titas
            their voices traveling to me
            tinny   ringing
            as if from yesterday's nova

familiar just
        what it sounds like
family
        blood
home
        marrow
bone
        grit
calcified memories
                of things that feel good
                            & heavy
            calcified
                as in made stronger by mountain sun
            only to have them crumble
                after enough time has passed
            (just like the mountain forgot what it used to be)

        still

it feels good to cook rice

it feels good to eat rice even by myself

& it feels familiar to know

       with each grain I swallow

I strap myself to my own

              heavy

     hunger

ACKNOWLEDGMENTS

Thank you to the editors of the following publications, in which these poems first appeared:

Apogee: "Lean Economy"

DIAGRAM: "I Sing Despite the Tender Stench Outside"

Diode: "Intake," "names are spells & I have four—"

EX/POST Magazine: "Piyesta"

Fugue: "What Does Death Feel Like Coming from a Woman?," "Snapshots of Girl with Galaxy of Spiders Drowning in Sopas"

Guernica: "when I say hello to the oldest apples"

The Margins: "When a Woman is Ugly"

Michigan Quarterly Review: Mixtape: "Yesterday's Traumas, Today's Salt"

Nat. Brut: "Chimera"

New England Review: "Bitter Melon"

Oxford Review of Books: "When I Sing to Myself, Who Listens?"

Poetry Northwest: "my childhood is a country of thieves—," "Perishable"

Poetry: "Hibiscus Dream No. 4"

Raleigh Review: "Ritual for Sickness"

Sundress Publications, 2018 Broadside Contest winner: an earlier version of "Feast"

TLDTD: "When They Gleam, When They Clatter"

Tupelo Quarterly: "I dream in a tongue other than my own"

Underblong: "Infinitives," "Milk"

Waxwing: "Birthstone," "It Feels Good to Cook Rice," "Soiled," "Triptych with Cityscape," "Watch Animals Closely for Strange Behavior"

Wildness: "Terrible Bodies"

Zoeglossia: "To the Boy Who Walks Backwards Everywhere He Goes"

Decade of the Brain: Poems, Janine Joseph

American Treasure, Jill McDonough

We Borrowed Gentleness, J. Estanislao Lopez

Brother Sleep, Aldo Amperán

Sugar Work, Katie Marya

Museum of Objects Burned by the Souls in Purgatory, Jeffrey Thomson

Constellation Route, Matthew Olzmann

How to Not Be Afraid of Everything, Jane Wong

Brocken Spectre, Jacques J. Rancourt

No Ruined Stone, Shara McCallum

The Vault, Andrés Cerpa

White Campion, Donald Revell

Last Days, Tamiko Beyer

If This Is the Age We End Discovery, Rosebud Ben-Oni

Pretty Tripwire, Alessandra Lynch

Inheritance, Taylor Johnson

The Voice of Sheila Chandra, Kazim Ali

Arrow, Sumita Chakraborty

Country, Living, Ira Sadoff

Hot with the Bad Things, Lucia LoTempio

Witch, Philip Matthews

Neck of the Woods, Amy Woolard

Little Envelope of Earth Conditions, Cori A. Winrock

Aviva-No, Shimon Adaf, Translated by Yael Segalovitz

Half/Life: New & Selected Poems, Jeffrey Thomson

Odes to Lithium, Shira Erlichman

Here All Night, Jill McDonough

To the Wren: Collected & New Poems, Jane Mead

Angel Bones, Ilyse Kusnetz

Monsters I Have Been, Kenji C. Liu

Soft Science, Franny Choi

Bicycle in a Ransacked City: An Elegy, Andrés Cerpa

Anaphora, Kevin Goodan

Ghost, like a Place, Iain Haley Pollock

Alice James Books is committed to publishing books that matter. The press was founded in 1973 in Boston, Massachusetts as a cooperative, wherein authors performed the day-to-day undertakings of the press. This element remains present today, as authors who publish with the press are invited to collaborate closely in the publication process of their work. AJB remains committed to its founders' original feminist mission, while expanding upon the scope to include all voices and poets who might otherwise go unheard. In keeping with its efforts to build equity and increase inclusivity in publishing and the literary arts, AJB seeks out poets whose writing possesses the range, depth, and ability to cultivate empathy in our world and to dynamically push against silence. The press was named for Alice James, sister to William and Henry, whose extraordinary gift for writing went unrecognized during her lifetime.

Designed by Alban Fischer

Printed by McNaughton & Gunn